STRESS
LESS

HOW TO STOP
FREAKING OUT AND
LIVE LIFE TO THE FULL

Jasmin Kirkbride

STRESS LESS

An Hachette UK Company
www.hachette.co.uk

Vie Books, an imprint of Summersdale Publishers Ltd
Part of Octopus Publishing Group Limited
Carmelite House
50 Victoria Embankment
LONDON
EC4Y 0DZ
UK

www.summersdale.com

Printed and bound in India

ISBN: 978-1-84953-910-4

Substantial discounts on bulk quantities of Summersdale books are available to corporations, professional associations and other organisations. For details contact general enquiries: telephone: +44 (0) 1243 771107 or email: enquiries@summersdale.com.

To..

From..

INTRODUCTION

TAKING THE FIRST STEPS

Bravery is turning to face the things I fear, not having no fears to face.

It's very unusual for anyone to go through life without feeling stressed out, anxious or afraid. If things get on top of you, you might feel overwhelmed with the strain and tension and your mind may travel to some rather dark places.

Deciding to face your anxieties head on can feel daunting, but looking after your mental health doesn't have to be intimidating. There are lots of simple things you can do to prevent and control stress and worry. The tips and advice in this book might not make you feel better overnight, but they will help you on your own personal journey to de-stress and live life to the full.

Mighty oaks from little acorns grow.

Anonymous

PART ONE

UNDERSTANDING FEAR, STRESS AND ANXIETY

To release stress, first I need to understand where it comes from.

People feel anxious and stressed about all sorts of things. Sometimes, you can identify the exact source, and other times you may just experience a general sense of unease. But don't be concerned; both these situations are very common, and even if you can't pinpoint your worry exactly there are plenty of things you can do to help your mind and body relax.

Before we talk about how to de-stress and dial down anxiety, it's important to know that they don't mean the same thing and that both are separate from fear – even if they all feel very similar.

It's alright to have butterflies in your stomach. Just get them to fly in formation.

Rob Gilbert

UNDERSTANDING FEAR

Fear is what you feel when something is threatening you directly. For example, if you're crossing a road and a car suddenly approaches, you'll feel afraid. This is your body going into what's known as 'fight or flight' mode, in which you automatically react and either try to resist the dangerous situation or to get away from it. After the danger has passed, your body returns to its normal state.

Feeling a degree of fear in objectively dangerous or threatening scenarios is a healthy response. It's what kept our ancestors alive when woolly mammoths were roaming the earth – and it's what makes you run instinctively when you see a car coming towards you!

SOME FEAR IS HEALTHY AND NORMAL, BUT IT'S IMPORTANT FOR ME TO DISTINGUISH BETWEEN A FEAR AND AN ANXIETY.

UNDERSTANDING STRESS

Stress is similar to fear, but it happens in situations that put us under emotional or mental strain. We feel stressed when we can't cope with the amount of pressure we're under and we experience uncomfortable, fear-like feelings.

Everybody experiences stress differently. Some people feel very stressed if they have to go on stage; for others it's taking tests. Emotional stress is associated with big life changes like moving house. Different people can cope with different amounts of pressure before they start to feel stressed. As with fear, people often find that when the stressful event is over their stress disappears and they can relax.

Some stress in life is inevitable, but consistently high levels of stress can be damaging to your physical and mental health – and can cause anxiety.

DON'T GO THROUGH LIFE; GROW THROUGH LIFE.

Eric Butterworth

A SITUATION MIGHT BE STRESSFUL, BUT I CAN CHOOSE TO STEP BACK AND RELAX AT ANY TIME.

UNDERSTANDING ANXIETY

Anxiety is actually quite different from stress, even though it makes you feel similar. The difference is what sets the feeling off in the first place.

Anxiety happens when you're unduly worried about something that isn't directly threatening you in the present moment. Taking an exam might be stressful; worrying for weeks beforehand about failing the exam is anxiety. A lot of people say they're stressed when what they really mean is that they're anxious. It's important to understand this difference because it'll help you identify your feelings so you can work out the best way to deal with them.

The man who removes a mountain begins by carrying away small stones.

Chinese proverb

IF EVERYBODY THOUGHT THE SAME AS ME, IMAGINE HOW BORING LIFE WOULD BE.

WHAT IS 'NORMAL' ANYWAY?

The term 'anxiety' covers a variety of states, ranging from the sensation of butterflies once in a while, to full-blown anxiety attacks. Everybody has wobbly patches at some point in their life, and that's totally OK because we all have our own journey to take. Having a mental-health condition doesn't make you 'crazy' or 'abnormal'. It's not a question of what's 'normal'; it's a question of what's uncomfortable and limiting for you. Is your anxiety getting in the way of life? Is it stopping you from socialising with friends or achieving your goals? If so, then it's time to take a proper look at it.

Sometimes a bad patch passes all by itself. In other cases, people experience longer-term mental-health difficulties that need more attention. If you're worried that there might be something more serious going on for you, here are several anxiety-related issues to look out for.

Normality is a paved road: it's comfortable to walk, but no flowers grow on it.

Vincent van Gogh

GENERALISED ANXIETY DISORDER (GAD)

People who suffer from Generalised Anxiety Disorder don't worry about one specific thing but many different things at different times. They may be unable to pinpoint the exact source of their worry, experiencing a general sense of unease. Often they're anxious most days and they might struggle to remember when they last felt relaxed. Common symptoms of GAD include feeling restless or nervous, and having trouble sleeping and concentrating.

BEING
POSITIVE
REQUIRES
COURAGE,
BUT I AM
COURAGEOUS.

When it gets too much,
I will always remember
to breathe.

ANXIETY ATTACKS

Anxiety attacks or panic attacks can happen just the once, every now and again, or regularly. Symptoms vary, but a lot of people report feeling dizzy, like they can't breathe, as if their heart is beating weirdly, and having tingly hands and feet. This is because anxiety attacks create an intense fight-or-flight response. It can feel so extreme that some sufferers worry they're dying during a panic attack. The truth is, no matter how awful they may feel, anxiety attacks aren't physically harmful and you can't die from them.

The best way to deal with panic attacks is to breathe slowly. Breathe in for four seconds, hold your breath for two seconds, breathe out for six seconds, hold for two seconds. Repeat this and count along steadily as you do so. Keep going with the breathing pattern until the panic passes. If possible, sit down with a glass of water and a low-sugar snack. Take it easy until you start to feel better.

OBSESSIVE–COMPULSIVE DISORDER (OCD)

Obsessive-compulsive disorder is a condition where people feel compelled to check things, to go through very specific routines, or to have certain thoughts over and over again.

The thoughts, checks and routines don't always make sense to the outside observer, but for the person with OCD they're very important and not being able to do them can be upsetting and cause anxiety. Interestingly, most OCD sufferers know that what they're doing doesn't really make sense but they feel unable to stop the cycle.

Our minds develop habits as well as our bodies, but it is still possible to break them.

OUR BIGGEST FEARS CAN BE THE SMALLEST THINGS; **THE TRICK** IS TO PUT THEM INTO **PERSPECTIVE.**

PHOBIAS

A phobia is a long-term, irrational fear of an object or situation, and it can cause someone distress and anxiety. Many phobias have their own particular names – for example, 'arachnophobia' is a fear of spiders.

Many people are afraid of spiders, but those with arachnophobia experience that fear to an unusually high degree. It may be that even talking about spiders makes their heart race and brings them out in a sweat. People suffering from phobias often find that their fears affect their day-to-day lives. Someone who is afraid of buttons might avoid wearing any clothes with buttons on, for instance. Such avoidance can make life and social situations tricky for phobia sufferers.

I AM EVERYTHING I'VE BEEN THROUGH, AND THAT'S WHAT MAKES ME UNIQUE.

POST-TRAUMATIC STRESS DISORDER (PTSD)

Post-traumatic stress disorder can be traced back to a disturbing physical or emotional experience, like an assault, a car crash or fighting in a war. Not everybody who experiences a traumatic event will experience PTSD, and it's rare in children. People who develop PTSD might suffer from flashbacks or memory loss, insomnia, bursts of anger and jumpiness.

LOOKING AFTER YOUR MENTAL HEALTH

These mental-health issues can be addressed and treated with the right help. If any conditions or symptoms seem familiar, or if you're ever totally overwhelmed and feel like you just can't escape your troubling thoughts, you can always seek out professional help.

Organise a trip to your doctor to talk about your situation. Your doctor will advise on the best plan of action for you and counselling might be a good option to get you back on your feet. There's more on where to find help at the end of the book.

A problem shared is a problem halved.

Proverb

WHEN THINGS GET TOUGH, I CAN ALWAYS REACH OUT FOR HELP.

PART TWO

CAUSES OF ANXIETY AND STRESS

Worrying about a problem makes
it seem bigger than it is.

Anxiety and stress can have any number of causes, from significant life events, such as moving house, to smaller day to day worries that build up over time. But, whether your worries are big or small, identifying the root of these feelings is the first step to managing them in a healthy way.

Here are a few of the most common reasons that people experience stress and anxiety – and some tips on how to help lessen their effects.

TURN YOUR FACE
TO THE SUN AND
THE SHADOWS
FALL BEHIND YOU.

Maori proverb

I HAVE THE POWER TO WRITE MY OWN STORY AND CREATE MY OWN SUCCESS.

EXAMS AND INTERVIEWS

A rush of adrenaline can help you out in the moment, but knowing an exam or interview is looming can drag you down for weeks if you fixate on it. When you feel that anxiety start – whether it's about failing the exam or forgetting to take something important to the interview – take a few deep, slow breaths.

Examine the story your anxiety is telling you and phrase it in a more positive light. For example, 'I'm going to fail because I've failed past exams' might turn into 'I've had some trouble in the past but I'm going to try my best and I can do well this time'.

CHANGE AND MOVING ON

Change in any context, whether you're moving house or changing colleges or jobs, can be causes of anxiety and stress. We're programmed to worry about change because early man had to be on high alert in unfamiliar landscapes. It's unlikely you're going to need to fight a bear when you walk into a new office, however, so nowadays it's less useful. To beat the stress, start by breathing deeply and slowly. Picture yourself in the new environment, settled and happy, after the change has been made, and tell yourself that everything is going to be OK. In fact, it will probably be even better!

I should always allow
for unforeseen positive
possibilities.

THE FIRST STEP TO BEING LOVED IS TO LOVE MYSELF.

SOCIAL ANXIETY

Do I look OK? Did I say the wrong thing? Does everyone think I'm an idiot? Thoughts like these are signs of social anxiety, which is a very common problem, especially for young people, and can be really painful to experience. Severe social anxiety can affect your work life, friendships, desire to pick up the phone or even leave the house. It can make you feel lonely and isolated.

One of the most helpful treatments for social anxiety is Cognitive Behavioural Therapy (CBT), which is about getting into the habit of thinking neutral or positive things instead of the negative ones produced by your anxiety. For instance, if you keep telling yourself 'These people are going to think I'm stupid', switch it round to 'These people are going to think I'm a new and interesting person'.

The enemy is fear. We think it is hate; but it is fear.

Mahatma Gandhi

SOMETIMES IT'S GOOD TO GO OFFLINE AND EXPERIENCE THE HERE AND NOW.

SOCIAL MEDIA ANXIETY

Just to be clear, Social Media Anxiety isn't a recognised medical condition – yet! But researchers are turning their attention more and more to social media's effects on our mental health. Social media isn't a bad thing in itself, and is a great way to connect with people and stay in touch with friends. However, it's a good idea to develop a few online habits to help you keep it light and fun.

BE YOURSELF.
EVERYONE ELSE
IS ALREADY
TAKEN.

Oscar Wilde

BY CHOOSING
TO BE MYSELF,
I'M OPENING
THE DOOR TO
THE THINGS
THAT I ENJOY.

FEAR OF MISSING OUT (FOMO)

We've all compared ourselves to other people on social media, spiralling down into the feeling that our lives aren't as cool, fun or exciting as theirs. You could be at home happily watching your way through a few episodes of a TV programme, when a photo of some friends at a party pops up on your newsfeed. Suddenly, your contented bubble has disappeared. Now you feel lonely and inadequate. We've all been there – FOMO is a beast.

Don't let FOMO win! Simply don't visit or follow the profiles of people who you know will make you feel bad or envious. Instead, regularly clear out your newsfeed to ensure that you're following people and pages with enjoyable and calming posts.

Also, keep in mind that people tend to post only the best bits on sites like Facebook, so online lives look much cooler than they really are. Offline, we're all as higgledy-piggledy as each other!

I'M BEAUTIFUL INSIDE AND OUT, AND I'M GOING TO SHINE MY LIGHT FOR EVERYONE TO SEE.

BUT EVERYONE ONLINE LOOKS LIKE...

Ever seen a photo of someone online then wanted to cover up your face or body because you think you don't look as good as them? You won't be the only one. The unrealistic expectations of the media and fashion industry have a lot to answer for, including contributing to rising rates of eating disorders and anxiety, which are starting at younger and younger ages.

If you feel yourself getting down, remind yourself that these standards are impossible and that many images in the mainstream media have been edited. The 'perfect' photos in adverts and magazines encourage many of us to enhance photos before posting them online – spots are erased, and filters are applied to make ourselves look more attractive, fitter and trendier than we are – when we're already perfect just the way we are in real life.

Still feeling anxious? Take a second to close your eyes, breathe and really reach out to your body with your mind. Give yourself a hug and tell yourself, in your head or out loud, that you're beautiful. Because – trust me – you are.

What we see depends mainly on what we look for.

John Lubbock

BREAK THE ADDICTION

Social media is addictive. Fact. Getting likes and notifications lights up all those juicy reward centres in your brain, making you crave them, so you check your accounts again and again throughout the day. These reward centres are also what make you feel sad when you don't get a like or any comments. Repeatedly logging into Facebook and other websites may make you feel like you're getting less interaction than you really are – and feeling you're not getting enough attention can inflict a dose of anxiety.

The advice on this is simple: log in less, and limit the amount of time you spend on social media when you do use it. To help you with this, delete all social media from your phone and download apps to your computer to limit the time you spend on certain websites. Remember to engage with the real, offline world!

I'M CHOOSING TO LIVE IN THE MOMENT BY TURNING OFF MY DEVICES AND SCREENS.

EMBRACE
YOUR JOURNEY

Whatever your state of mind, embrace your own personal journey. We can't go through life without experiencing times of change, movement and uncertainty, and often in these situations stress and anxiety is inevitable. But, although they can't be avoided, these feelings can be managed. It may sound cliché, but by acknowledging that you are going through a tough phase, and knowing that stress is a natural part of life's journey, you will reach a positive place more quickly than if you are constantly trying to resist how you feel.

When I treat myself with gentleness, the world becomes a kinder place. So I'm going to love myself – I'm doing the best I can.

PART THREE

MANAGING NEGATIVE THOUGHTS

I can change my world by choosing
to think positively.

The human mind is a creative little beast and, at times, it can come up with some really horrible ideas.

But when you're anxious, it's important to remember that your worst thoughts about yourself aren't necessarily true. This is especially the case for people suffering from anxiety, because an anxious person has formed a pattern of negative thinking. By breaking this habit, you can transform your life from the inside out. Here are a few tips on how to make the change.

Worrying is using your imagination to create something you don't want.

Esther Hicks

I KNOW AND UNDERSTAND THAT MY WORST THOUGHTS ARE OFTEN THE LEAST TRUE.

IDENTIFY NEGATIVE THOUGHTS

The first step towards transforming negative thoughts is to identify what they are. This can be quite a challenge; if you're finding it hard, try writing a diary.

Start to keep an honest, private diary and read back over it every week or so, looking out for the recurring thoughts that made you feel stressed or discouraged. These might include blaming yourself or feeling ashamed about things that aren't your fault or making something worse in your head than it actually was. Writing everything down will help you to put it into perspective and to focus on the good stuff.

NEGATIVE THOUGHTS, WHEREVER YOU COME FROM, **LEAVE ME ALONE!**

LET GO OF NEGATIVE THOUGHTS

When you're trying not to worry, it's common to try to push the bad thoughts away, to shove them out of your mind completely. Instead of resisting them, relax into your thoughts and let them move through your mind. By pushing negativity away, you're engaging with the thought and are likely to follow it up and keep thinking about it. It's much more effective to stand back and observe your negative thoughts, almost as if they belong to someone else, and let them move on like clouds in the sky. Don't cling to or push away your thoughts, just let them be, then let them pass.

If you have good thoughts, they will shine out of your face like sunbeams and you will always look lovely.

Roald Dahl

THINK POSITIVE

Do you feel overwhelmed by something? Is work piling up? Or are you worried about a big event that's looming on the horizon? Get into the habit of thinking nice or neutral things rather than the bad stuff you might be used to. When your worst thoughts strike, turn your inner voice around and make it tell you the positive, not the negative. Remove absolute terms like 'always' and 'never' from your everyday vocabulary. Define any difficult stuff in your life in terms that make it seem less intimidating and more manageable; a 'disaster' becomes a 'challenge' and something 'terrible' becomes 'unfortunate'.

Constantly thinking positive is hard, but keep at it and soon you won't even notice you're doing it. You'll be well on the way to a new mindset and becoming the brightest, happiest version of yourself!

Turning my thoughts around isn't always easy, but I know I can do it.

GO EASY
ON YOUR BRAIN

Positive thinking is like a muscle that you have to exercise – you're training your brain to think differently. Retraining doesn't happen overnight, and getting rid of negative thoughts takes time and practice, so if you slip up occasionally be gentle and patient with yourself. Don't give yourself a hard time because being anxious about being anxious isn't helpful. Instead, give yourself a mental cuddle, forgive yourself and move on. You'll beat that nagging thought next time. Positivity starts right here and right now!

Feelings are much like waves; we can't stop them from coming, but we can choose which ones to surf.

Jonatan Mårtensson

PART FOUR

BREATHING

I'm going to breathe deep and
allow my body and mind
to become one.

You may have noticed that we've already begun to talk about breathing. Breathing is something that your body does automatically, and most of the time we don't even notice it, but did you know that how you breathe can make a big difference to how you feel?

You don't have to pay attention to your breathing every minute of the day, but here are a couple of breathing exercises to help you chill out when you're stressed out.

BREATHING IN, I CALM MY BODY. BREATHING OUT, I SMILE.

Thích Nhất Hạnh

BY PAYING
ATTENTION TO
MY BREATH, I'M
HELPING TO CALM
MY BODY. BY PAYING
ATTENTION TO
THE MOMENT, I'M
HELPING MYSELF
TO LIVE IN THE
HERE AND NOW.

BASIC BREATHING

This is a great exercise for grounding yourself during overwhelming moments. It can be done anywhere, but it works best if you're sitting or standing still. Close your eyes, then breathe in through your nose and out through your mouth in a slow pattern: in for three seconds, hold for two, out for three seconds, hold for two.

Repeat for at least ten breaths (or for longer if you want), focusing on the sensation of breathing. Let your tummy soften and your lower ribs expand outwards, as if you're trying to breathe into your stomach rather than your upper chest. Consciously relax your body and don't force the breath – just let it happen naturally.

THE WORLD MAY SEEM FAST, BUT IF I SLOW DOWN, THE WORLD WILL SLOW DOWN WITH ME.

EQUAL BREATHING

This one takes a little time and practice, but it's great for slowing down the body and shrugging off a stressful day. It should be done in a quiet space, where you can sit comfortably. This exercise should be done with caution, as breathing in this manner can make you feel faint if you push yourself too hard.

Just as before, close your eyes and breathe into your belly. This time though, gently make the in and out breaths slightly longer every time, starting with three seconds each way. You should never hold the breath, but let it flow in and out. Stop extending your breath when you feel you've reached a comfortable limit and stay with that level for ten breaths, before moving on and returning to your life.

PART FIVE

MINDFULNESS

My mind is a beautiful machine.
If it starts going off course,
I can rewire it.

Think meditation is all about hippies in harem pants humming and sitting cross-legged on the floor? Think again! Many of the principles of meditation have influenced mindfulness, which trains your mind to think clearly and positively. Mindfulness is like ballast on a ship: the more you put in, the more balanced you'll stay even in the stormiest of seas.

There are many ways to practise mindfulness, here are just a few to help you on your way. You don't have to practise every day but, as with playing a musical instrument, the more you practise, the easier and more natural it becomes. If you like what you find here, there are plenty of apps and online videos that offer mindfulness tips and courses.

If we practise mindfulness, we always have a place to be when we are afraid.

Thích Nhất Hạnh

IT IS OK TO
LET THINGS
GO SIMPLY
BECAUSE THEY
ARE HEAVY.

BE IN THE HERE AND NOW

Social-media mayhem exploding on your screens? Deadlines looming? One of the best things you can do when the going gets really tough is to take a little break. Make space every day to give ten minutes to yourself. This practice isn't about trying to make the moment 'perfect' or about not thinking; it's about appreciating the present moment and really being here.

Turn your screens off, put your phone on silent and go to a quiet place where you can sit comfortably. Relax your eyelids so they're not quite closed, straighten your back without straining and keep your belly soft. Breathe deeply into your belly, just as you did in the breathing exercises, and focus on how your breath feels. After a few moments, spread your senses outwards, notice the sounds around you, the feel of the floor or seat beneath you. Just sit in the moment, let your mind hang loose and let your thoughts pass through you without judgement.

SOMETIMES MY ANXIETY MAKES ME AFRAID OF MY OWN MIND, BUT IF I LET MYSELF RELAX IT BECOMES A SAFE SPACE.

BODY SCAN

If you're in the habit of worrying, it might be difficult to trust yourself not to get stressed. But you can get back in touch with your brain and body, and trust them to be positive.

In a still, quiet space, sit comfortably or lie down. Breathe in deep and centre yourself. Relax. Move your awareness right down to your toes. When you next breathe in, imagine you're breathing right into your feet. As you breathe out, consciously relax your toes and imagine that you're breathing out all your stress. Repeat this all the way up your body, relaxing each part as you go: your ankles, calves, knees, thighs, hips, tummy, ribs, chest, arms, hands, fingers, neck and face. As in previous exercises, watch your thoughts like they're clouds in the sky, without either grasping at them or pushing them away. Breathe around them as they pass through you, and know that all will be well.

Instead of 'Let it go', we should probably say 'Let it be'.

Jon Kabat-Zinn

I LOVE MYSELF
UNCONDITIONALLY.
JUST BEING ME
IS MORE THAN
ENOUGH.

COMPASSION

Many people suffering from anxiety and stress struggle with feelings of worthlessness. Am I attractive or clever? Do these people like me? Am I working hard enough? These sorts of negative questions only make our worries worse.

Compassion is important in turning the anxiety boat around, but it can be challenging because it involves learning to love yourself unconditionally. Compassion is love, but it's not romantic. It's a universal feeling of kindness towards everything – most importantly, in this case, yourself.

Being compassionate towards yourself isn't about buying things, or being selfish; it means taking the pressure off, and being caring towards yourself and your body. It's like a mental hug. Try purposefully feeling love for yourself once a day every day, and see how quickly you start feeling better.

OUR SORROWS AND WOUNDS ARE HEALED ONLY WHEN WE TOUCH THEM WITH COMPASSION.

Buddha

PART SIX

SLEEPING

Tomorrow holds the unknown, but
it always manages to look after itself
when it becomes today.

When you're exhausted from worrying, there's nothing worse than not being able to get to sleep. On average we need about eight hours' sleep a night, and having at least a couple of those before midnight is ideal.

Sleep is crucial for the body to relax and de-stress, but when you're worried it can be one of the hardest things to achieve. Here are several tips to help yourself get more – and better quality – sleep.

Sleep is the best meditation.

Dalai Lama

TURN OFF THE SCREENS

OK, this is a big one: stay away from screens for at least an hour before bed. The blue light given out by LED and TV screens tricks your brain into thinking it's still daytime and that you aren't sleepy yet. Actually, you might be exhausted, but you wouldn't realise until you stopped looking at the screen. This artificial light makes your brain more active in general, meaning it takes you longer to wind down once you do get to bed.

You can download apps that dim your device's screen with a red tint which counters the blue light the later it gets. But to really allow your brain to get ready for sleep, just turn off the tech!

I'm completely free to become who I need to be.

BEDTIME ROUTINE

Bedtime routines aren't just for kids! Having a set routine before bed trains your mind and body to expect sleep and also lets your body know that sleep is a safe activity, which is beneficial for those with anxiety.

Try to get to bed around the same time every night. Turn off your screens and sounds. Maybe have a cup of herbal, non-caffeinated tea, but stay away from hot chocolate and other sugary drinks as they'll make you buzz for hours. Brush your teeth and wash your face, adding in a bath or shower if you want. Snuggle up in bed and take some time to unwind. Maybe you want to read a book or perhaps this is the time you write in your diary; just make sure you pick a non-digital activity. When you start to get drowsy, close your book or diary, turn the light off and settle down.

It can take a while for the body to get used to a new routine, so keep at it and soon you'll be getting to sleep in no time.

I CHOOSE TO
RELAX AND
TRUST THAT
EVERYTHING
WILL WORK
OUT, WHETHER I
HAVE CONTROL
OVER IT OR
NOT. IT WILL.

SLEEP IS NOT A DESTINATION; IT'S JUST ANOTHER PART OF THE JOURNEY.

CHANGE THE WAY YOU THINK ABOUT SLEEP

When sleep is evading us, it can seem like a faraway destination that's difficult to reach. But when you're fully relaxed, sleep is a very natural state for your body to fall into and you don't have to work for it. In fact, the more you struggle to sleep, the more your body will tense and your mind will worry. Let go of trying to get to sleep and trust that your body knows how to get there – it always does eventually.

Today has been
a good, full day.
Now I'm allowed
to sleep.

BREATHE OUT THOUGHTS, BREATHE IN SLEEP

If you're having trouble calming your mind once the lights are out, try some mindfulness practices – body scans are particularly helpful at bedtime. If you find that's not enough, give this exercise a go.

Lying comfortably, consciously relax your body, close your eyes and breathe deeply and slowly into your belly. Feel the air as it moves through your nose or mouth, down your throat and into your lungs, then follow its journey back out again. Allow thoughts to crop up when they want to but, instead of getting involved in them, visualise them becoming part of your breath. As you exhale, let the thoughts go with your breath, and imagine yourself in a state of relaxation and calm. Allow yourself to recognise that you've worked hard today and deserve a proper rest tonight.

PART SEVEN

RELAXATION

Unwind, release, let go.
I trust the world to catch me
when I stop worrying.

Getting wound up? Is your day becoming stressful? Don't wait until you're on the edge of a panic attack to do something about it. Use these relaxation techniques to bring yourself back down to earth as soon as you feel yourself tensing up.

RELEASE YOUR
STRUGGLE, LET
GO OF YOUR MIND,
THROW AWAY YOUR
CONCERNS AND
RELAX INTO
THE WORLD.

Dan Millman

If you have a flat tyre, that is also part of the journey.

Chögyam Trungpa

PLAYTIME

One of the top reasons people get stressed is too much work and not enough play. There will be times in your life when you need to work hard, but even then it's essential to take time out and play. Paint, see a movie, read a novel – take time to do something just for the pleasure and enjoyment of it. Remember also to take time to make contact with your family and friends. Spending time with the people you love is another great way to unwind and have fun.

WHEN I ALLOW
MYSELF TO DO
THE THINGS I
LOVE WITHOUT
PRESSURE
OR GOALS,
MY BODY CAN
TRULY RELAX.

VISUALISATION

When it all gets a bit much, take a minute out to picture yourself in a safe, happy environment, perhaps a field, a beach or a library. It can be real or imagined – the important thing is that it's a place where you feel safe and loved.

Visualise the details about your place: are there flowers in your field, or is there sand on your beach? What books are on the shelves in your library? Think about the sounds and sensations you might encounter, like birdsong or a gentle breeze. Focus on the feelings you experience in your safe place.

Remember: this is your happy place. It's exactly what you want and need it to be, and you can visit it whenever you want.

WHEREVER I AM,
I HAVE A SAFE
PLACE TO GO.

ACUPRESSURE

There are pressure points all over your body which have different effects when you stimulate them. Some of the easiest pressure points to find are on your temples and in your hands. These are simple, in-the-moment exercises you can do anywhere to help you relax.

To ease tension, find the flat parts on either side of your head beside your eyes. Apply gentle pressure with two or three fingers, and rub in slow circles. Carry on for about two minutes, changing direction halfway through.

For de-stressing, use the pressure points in your hands. Squeeze the fleshy, webbed bit of skin between your thumb and forefinger, getting as close to the place where the bones meet as you can. Hold for two minutes, then repeat on the other hand.

LAUGHTER IS THE BEST MEDICINE.

Proverb

LAUGHTER

Laughing actively lowers your body's stress levels and encourages your brain to release happy chemicals. It's genuinely, scientifically excellent for you.

If there's no one around to crack a joke with, try watching a funny video, listening to an amusing podcast or reading a laugh-out-loud book. You could even give a laughter yoga class a try. Just make sure you LOL as often as possible!

WHEN I LAUGH, I WILL REALLY LET GO AND ENJOY THE MOMENT.

Why not just live in the moment, especially if it has a good beat?

Goldie Hawn

CRANK UP THE VOLUME

Feeling stress building up inside you? Think you might pop like a balloon if you don't do something right now? Then turn on some tunes and blast the music. Cheery, happy songs work best – ones that you can dance or sing along to. Or, if you're in a quieter mood, try something soft but upbeat. Music is great for your mind, so rock on to bliss out!

FIND SOME SUNSHINE AND LIE IN IT. IT'S THE GREATEST MEDICINE IN THE WORLD – AND IT'S FREE.

SEEK OUT NATURE

Getting outside, away from concrete and into nature has a positive effect on your mental state. Go somewhere you can feel the grass under your feet and the wind on your face; winter or summer, fresh air and green time do you so much good.

Whether you're at the beach or in a forest, take time to appreciate the little details – the sunshine through the leaves or the sound of the waves. Relax your walk to an amble, take the day as it comes and feel your worries being blown away.

AS SOON AS YOU TRUST YOURSELF, YOU WILL KNOW HOW TO LIVE.

Johann Wolfgang von Goethe

TAKE A BATH

A long, hot bath is like chicken soup for the soul. The sensation of being warm and in water allows your body to totally relax and release all its tension. Adding in bubbles and lighting a few candles (safely away from your hair!) will give a sense of luxury. A decent bath is a real treat and an excellent way to care for yourself.

After a bath, your body takes 15–30 minutes to cool down – take this time to wind down and recoup. Dry off, wrap yourself in a warm blanket or duvet, curl up in a comfortable place and enjoy this moment.

Positivity is physical as well as mental. By treating my body, I'm treating my mind – and they'll both be grateful.

MUDDY WATER LET
STAND BECOMES
CLEAR.

Lao Tzu

WRITE IT OUT

When all your feelings are piling up, it can be cathartic to set them down on paper. Start keeping a regular diary, allowing yourself to write freely about anything and everything for ten minutes each day. Include this as part of your bedtime routine and it'll help you deal with your day and put it to bed before you head there yourself.

Aim to finish every entry with a couple of lines about something you're grateful for – whether it was a tasty sandwich at lunch or sunshine through the trees – because a little daily gratitude will help build your positivity powerhouse!

BY WRITING MY WORRIES DOWN, I CAN LOOK AT THEM FROM ANOTHER PERSPECTIVE AND THEN SAY, 'ENOUGH. NOW GO AWAY.'

MAKE A LIST

When work is snowballing and you can't see the end of the road, it's time to make a list. Write down everything you have to do on a piece of paper, breaking it down into achievable, bite-sized tasks. Highlight the things that are most important and work your way through those first, ticking them off as you go. Then return to the top of the list and check the tasks off one by one.

The simple act of writing out your to-do list helps to put everything in perspective. Remember: there's no task so big it can't be completed. Just focus on the next step in front of you.

I am not afraid of storms,
for I am learning how
to sail my ship.

Louisa May Alcott

NINETY-NINE
PER CENT OF
THE THINGS I'M
WORRIED ABOUT
WILL NEVER
HAPPEN. IT'S OK
TO CHILL OUT.

IT'S OK

There's a lot of power in simply telling yourself that it's OK, you're OK, everything is going to be OK.

Anxiety sufferers may be subconsciously afraid that something bad will happen if they stop worrying, but this couldn't be further from the truth; the future will happen whether you worry about it or not, and it generally works out better than worriers think it will. It's OK to let go. Everything is going to work out well in the end – and it's OK to believe that too.

DON'T WORRY ABOUT THE WORLD COMING TO AN END TODAY. IT IS ALREADY TOMORROW IN AUSTRALIA.

PART EIGHT

WELL-BEING

Eat better, not less. Move
more, beat stress!

The saying 'You are what you eat' is definitely true! When you don't feed your body the nutrition it needs, it feels under pressure and run down, worsening both physical and mental stress. Eating well and getting a decent amount of exercise really boosts your well-being, including your mental health.

Exercise helps to fight the symptoms of stress by increasing concentration levels and releasing endorphins, serotonin and dopamine – your body's happy hormones. Movement helps to physically tire you out, so you're more likely to sleep better at night while feeling more active and awake during the day.

Happiness is not a goal… it's a by-product of a life well lived.

Eleanor Roosevelt

I AM STRONGER THAN MY CRAVINGS.

THINGS TO AVOID

When we're stressed, there can be a real temptation to binge-eat or, conversely, to not eat at all. Neither of these is good for fighting negative thoughts. Eating lots of saturated fat and sugary foods will give you crashes and make you feel lethargic, while keeping vital nutrients from your body will only make you feel lower.

Be careful what you drink too. Although caffeine may hype you up in the short-term, once it's worn off it can cause drowsiness and grumpiness, and will interrupt your natural sleeping patterns. Say no to booze, which is a depressant.

Coming off these types of food and drink can make you feel rough in the first few days because they're all slightly addictive, but be disciplined and you'll soon notice a difference in the way you think and feel.

EAT HEALTHILY

Turn away from the junk-food aisle and pick up some fruit and veg – they may not seem as appetising at first, but your body will thank you for it. Aim to eat at least your five a day of fruit and vegetables, with slow-burning carbohydrates like wholegrain rice or pasta on the side. Mix in some proteins – like nuts, meat, dairy, eggs and particularly fish, which is full of great, stress-busting nutrients.

Ensure that all the right vitamins and minerals are included in your diet too (if in doubt, try some supplements to top you up). The antioxidant vitamins A, C and E will help combat the symptoms of stress. Vitamins D and B will boost your mood. Take care of your eating habits and you're well on your way to a happier body, a stronger immune system and a healthier mind.

**When I eat well,
I feel well.**

WORK ON WHAT
IS REAL RATHER
THAN WORRY
ABOUT WHAT IS
UNREAL.

Elizabeth George

Sometimes when I'm feeling stressed, all I need to level myself out is a glass of water and a snack.

DRINK PLENTY OF WATER

Fruit juice and fizzy pop might taste great but they have a high sugar content. The best thing you can drink is pure water. Water is amazing for your body: it helps your skin stay healthy and pimple-free, it makes all your organs run smoothly, and it helps keep your brain hydrated for thinking positively and staying focused. Water really is a miracle drink.

Non-caffeinated herbal teas can be very beneficial too and many have their own unique qualities. For example, chamomile is great for helping you sleep, while peppermint is good for calming the stomach. If you're missing coffee, ginger tea gives you a natural zing to keep you going throughout the day.

IF I FEEL MY
TUMMY TIGHTEN,
I BREATHE IN
GENTLY AND
TELL MYSELF
EVERYTHING IS
GOING TO BE OK.

IS YOUR STOMACH STRESSED?

When stressed or anxious, some of us experience tightness in the tummy that makes us feel like we don't want to eat. This link between stress and stomach pain is sometimes so strong that it might be diagnosed by a doctor as Irritable Bowel Syndrome (IBS), a harmless but sore condition.

To help ease these tummy troubles, try slowly sipping a cup of peppermint tea before a meal. Eat soft, well-cooked foods if you find raw food hard to handle, and stay away from fatty foods, which are tricky to digest. Take time out to eat away from your desk, sitting down in a peaceful space. Wear warm, comfortable clothes which are loose around the waist and belly. You could also try holding a hot water bottle to your lower back. As you relax, so will your tummy.

Feelings are just visitors. Let them come and go.

Mooji

EXERCISE

Exercise can seem rather intimidating, with all those gym-goers in their trainers doing fancy things with weights and running machines, but exercise just means movement. You don't have to do hardcore workouts (unless you want to) – there are plenty of other options – and it doesn't have to be boring or difficult.

Keep it fun by finding a sport or exercise you love and teaming up with a friend to support each other. YouTube has loads of free exercise videos if you want to connect to an online fitness community, or you could join a local sports club. Set aside two or three hour-long sessions per week to work out and do a little something to exercise every day, even if it's just a ten-minute walk down the road. Remember to breathe in deep to really get all the oxygenating benefits of fresh air to your brain!

MOTIVATION
WILL GET ME
STARTED; HABIT
WILL KEEP
ME GOING.

MINDFUL MOVEMENT

Gentle exercises that can be practised with mindfulness are effective at combating stress and worry because they encourage you to get in touch with yourself. Swimming, yoga, Pilates and t'ai chi all use rhythmic breathing patterns to align the body and mind, bringing you back down to earth, to the here and now. If you can't get to the local gym or pool, search for online yoga or t'ai chi tutorials, paying careful attention to your body as you exercise. Breathe in and out with awareness, letting your mind drop into that same, soft space you reach when you practise your mindfulness exercises.

My body and mind are so closely linked together that by helping one, I can make the other better.

I'M NOT ON A DIET, I'M NOT TRYING TO LOSE WEIGHT, I'M NOT TRYING TO CHANGE MY BODY. I'M SIMPLY TAKING CARE OF MYSELF.

MY BODY IS A TEMPLE

Don't fall into the trap of letting exercise and healthy eating become another thing to worry about. Taking care of yourself isn't about how you look – it's about how you feel. If there happen to be positive side effects on your appearance, then that's just the icing on the cake. Don't be hard on yourself if you slip up occasionally. Instead, remember that you're human and that everybody has a junk-food treat once in a while.

Approach what you eat and how you exercise with an open, compassionate mind. Don't push your body too far too fast, and appreciate how it works and the amazing things it does for you.

Life isn't about finding yourself. Life is about creating yourself.

George Bernard Shaw

PART NINE

TALKING AND FINDING HELP

I'm not alone and there's no shame in asking for help.

Talking about your stress and anxiety might seem daunting, but the truth is that your friends and family love you and they want to be there for you. It's a massive help to have someone around to support you and keep an eye out for when you might freak out.

Everyone discusses their problems differently: some do public status updates on Facebook while others are more private, preferring to confide in one or two people. Whatever your style is, approach your problems gently. Start small. Only reveal as many details as you want to – it's your call.

JUST BE YOURSELF. THERE IS NO ONE BETTER.

Taylor Swift

**By talking, I'm
opening myself up
to the possibility
of support.**

CREATE A SUPPORT NETWORK

Talking to people you love and trust about your worries will help you to feel secure and to build up the support network you need to live and enjoy your life to the full. Identify family or friends who you know you can rely on when the going gets tough and explain to them what you're going through. There is always someone who wants to listen to you.

A 'NO' IS JUST AS GOOD AS A 'YES'.

LEARN TO SAY 'NO'

Often the reason we're stressed out is that we've taken on too much or we're trying to please too many people. It's important to recognise when your plate is full and to stop piling on the work and activities – and to realise that 'no' is a very useful, positive word. Sometimes you just have to say 'no' in life, whether that means turning down a project or treating yourself to a night at home on the sofa.

Lay down your boundaries nicely but firmly. Anyone who is worth having in your life, whether it's a friend or a colleague, will understand. In fact, people may trust you more, because they'll appreciate that you're fully committed to the things you do say 'yes' to.

It's only by saying 'no' that you can concentrate on the things that are really important.

Steve Jobs

TOGETHER, WE CAN MAKE IT!

FRIENDS WITH ANXIETY

Once you start opening up about your issues, you might well find that other people are going through similar things – even if outwardly they seem to be coping brilliantly with absolutely everything that life throws at them – which can be an incredibly sharing and supportive experience.

As the friend or relative of someone suffering from stress or anxiety, the best thing you can do is to be there to listen. Be open and loving towards them, and treat them just as you'd want them to treat you if you were feeling fragile or in a difficult place.

THE BRAVE
MAN IS NOT
HE WHO
DOES NOT
FEEL AFRAID,
BUT HE WHO
CONQUERS
THAT FEAR.

Nelson Mandela

CONSIDER COUNSELLING

If it ever gets too much and you feel like you can't cope, you can always seek counselling. The best first step is to go to your doctor and talk to them confidentially about what's going on in your life. They might recommend that you see a counsellor, or they may give you some medication to help.

If your situation is urgent and you can't wait to see the doctor there are some excellent helplines you can call. To find out more, visit:

www.mind.org.uk
www.samaritans.org
www.anxietyuk.org.uk
www.turn2me.org

**Whatever's happening,
I can get through this,
and it's OK to ask for
help on the way.**

CONCLUSION

LOOKING AHEAD

The past has happened; the future will look after itself. I'm here right now, and that's all that matters.

Whenever you're going through a rough patch, concentrate on putting one foot in front of the other and on moving forward. A small step forward is still a step in the right direction. Congratulate yourself on every accomplishment. Breathe into your fear and it will evaporate. Face your worries and their shadows will shrink. Cut your stress down to size.

It takes a brave person to look at the things that scare them, but you have the courage to do this. Keep calm, keep positive and form new habits for a freer life, so you can be your biggest, brightest, happiest self.

Everything is OK in the end. If it's not OK, then it's not the end.

Anonymous

If you're interested in finding out more about our books, find us on Facebook at **Summersdale Publishers** and follow us on Twitter at **@Summersdale**.

www.summersdale.com

IMAGE CREDITS